After The Storm
Recovering from Personal Loss and Grief
Workbook/Journal
First Edition

By T. B. Williams

AFTER THE STORM
WORKBOOK/JOURNAL
First Edition

ISBN 13: 978-0-9793339-2-7
ISBN:10: 0-9793339-2-X
Published by FBT/MBSS PRODUCTIONS,LLC

© 2012 by T. B. Williams
Layout by A.T.B of FTB/MBSS
Carmen T. Milton of CTM Services/Editing Consultant

Scripture Quotations:
Scripture taken from the New King James Version
© 1979, 1980, 1982, By Thomas Nelson Inc. Used By Permission. All rights reserved.
ALL RIGHTS RESERVED
No part of this publication may be reproduced or stored in a retrieval system, or transmitted, in any form or by any means electronic, mechanical, photocopying, recording, or otherwise without written permission of the Author/Publisher. The intent of the Author/Publisher is to offer information in general towards your spiritual and emotional well-being, not to offer any medical advice or legal advice or prescription for treatment of any legal, physical, mental or medical problems. In the event you adhere to any of the information offered in this publication, which is your right under the constitution of the U.S. The Author/Publisher assumes no responsibility for your actions.
Request for information@:
P.O.Box 3066
Newport News, VA 23603
Printed in the U.S.A.

Contents

My Journey Through the Phases of Loss and Grief................1

And Now the Mourning (Phases 4 & 5)......................8

My Experience with Palliative Care..........................13

Recovering Emotionally After Loss..........................16

Emotional Healing Worksheet................................21

Journal..27

Introduction

Grief and Loss

Grief by definition per Encarta Dictionary/English North American version defines this word as (intense sorrow, great sadness, especially as a result of a death (loss)/cause of intense sorrow, deep and profound sorrow, especially a specific event or situation/trouble, annoyance).

As I have come to learn due to recent losses in my own life, and by way of intense research and much travail, the definition offered by the Encarta Dictionary presents a somewhat accurate account of this extreme emotional state that I am encountering, yet it does not quite offer solace in regards to my sometimes constant, sometimes deceitfully fleeting, and somehow reoccurring pain.

As a survivor of several losses, I have known grief to be a constant companion that can mask it's self in many forms. However, recently I had to deal with the loss of a parent....this brought on a grief unlike anything I have ever known before.

My story starts with a mother of whom I was estranged from for several years beginning in childhood. As I became an adult with children of my own, I tried to forge a relationship with my mother, but still it did not ever amount to the dream I wished realized (envisioned). Nevertheless, she was my mother by all means, and the underlying truth of who she was and what she was to me never diminished the value I placed in my heart for her.

Being estranged from my mother, caused me to experience grief on some level due to my issues surrounding the abandonment I felt by not having her around. However, her death created a precisely different aspect of grief due to the finality of it all. At the end of the day, the reality was before her death, I had the Hope of reconciliation. However, when death comes, not only does it kill the person, but it kills the Hope.

Today I want to regain Hope! Not only for myself, but for others who are experiencing losses as well. Whether it is the loss of a loved one, a job, a relationship, a divorce, a miscarriage, declining health issues, or anyone who may be suffering losses of any kind and feel as if the emotional weight they bear is more than they can take, or even understand. I want to offer hope, offer understanding, and offer an olive branch in the sharing of my story. I know that by helping others we help ourselves. And I would like to thank you today for helping me heal by letting me share my story, research, and struggle with you.

I pray that as you read through these pages you will find healing, deliverance, and comfort in knowing you are not alone, and to know the process that you are experiencing now is a normal one. I am no medical or clinical professional, neither am I a legal advisor, however, I now consider myself an End of Life Family Care/Education Advocate. While my mother was facing the end of her life, I really wish I had one around.

I remember sitting on the phone calling anyone who would listen, from funeral directors, to 211(community information hotlines). I even called road side assistance one day and was able to receive comfort. However, somehow God always had a ram in the bush, each time I called someone in an unexpected place, I received an unexpected but much needed comfort to make it through the day. And thus, **"After the Storm"** was born. I am now on my quest to offer that same comfort to others facing the *Storm* (the same set of circumstances).

My Story Through The Five Stages of Grief and Loss

In a book I read by Elisabeth Kübler-Ross, "On Death and Dying," there was an idea introduced by her that there are at least five stages of normal grief. She detailed the stages as **Bargaining, Anger, Denial and Isolation, Acceptance and Depression**.

For the purpose of this book I will call them phases. For me that was how I rationalized what I was going through, a "Phase", later I realized it was a condition called Grief. I must admit that I have at some point during the loss of my mother gone through all of these phases, and at times they still reoccur in no particular order or phase. There are times these phases seem more heart wrenching than other times. Still in all, it is a process and I am gradually still getting stronger because of it.

Throughout this workbook I will briefly discuss my experiences through each of these phases, and hopefully you will find this helpful. You might even see yourself through my experiences, but more than that, I want you to gain hope and strength in knowing that you do not walk alone. This process will at some time be a common thread for all of us who exist in this human form. You may have experienced these stages in the order that I have or maybe not at all. This is just to be used to open the conversation and maybe offer you hope and give you the strength to reach outside of yourself to get the help or guidance of professionals in your community if needed.

Once again I do not want to offer this as any kind of professional advice, but more so of a companion piece from one person to another as a source of connection. The purpose of this workbook is to offer an example to aid you in knowing that you are not the only one feeling the way you do, and to emphasize the fact that **you are not your loss**. You do have value and worth, and I hope that this will give you strength to move forward with your life. Where there is life there is hope, was a statement I made daily as my mother reached the end of her days, but now that she is gone, the Hope resides in me.

Dedication

To the kindness of strangers... to my family and friends! But to God and to my Mom the most!

Thanks to Ms. Boston-Davis and Prof. Graham for the long talks and words encouragement.

To Edwina, Gracie, Patrice, and Tyler, Thank You!

And to all the Attendees and Guest Speakers, Thank You!

Last but not least to LAW, AT, and Baby A & B!

My Journey Through the Phases of Loss and Grief

Phase 1- Bargaining:

In Hopes of trying to save ourselves from the impending doom that we fear, we come to the phase of **Bargaining**. In this phase we find ourselves making deals with God while hoping for a second chance, or even a miracle. We do not want to accept the verdict that has been passed down to us of death or impending death, or loss of any kind (Financial/Relational/Emotional). We bargain in hope to try to control the uncontrollable. In this stage we are oftentimes overwhelmed and have feelings of weakness in mind and strength. We feel vulnerable and move through the world like an open wound, leaking and oozing the issues of our lives. Even though we may bandage it up in pretty clothes and smiling faces, it still shines through in our actions and thoughts with second guesses of should have, would have, could have's, or if I would have done this, then maybe that.

I experienced this for myself, praying for miracles and saying all that I would do differently if my mother had recovered. I even mourned the Hope of what never was, or what could have been. As I stated in the introduction, my mother and I did not have the kind of relationship I Hoped for, however, I still had the Hope of one day having a good relationship while life still remained within her. But once death was my mother's fate, not only did it take my mother, but it also killed my Hope.

As I researched and read up on issues surrounding the area of grief, I found that this phase works as a defense mechanism implemented by our minds to protect us of the pain of our loss.

Are you able to identify with the Phase of Bargaining in relation to your personal loss?
_____
_____
_____
_____
_____

In what ways if any did it make you feel?
_____
_____
_____
_____
_____

After The Storm

Can you relate to Bargaining being used as a type of Defense Mechanism to protect you from your loss?
_____
_____
_____
_____

Phase 2 - Anger:

Why Me God, Why my Mother, Why Now? In rage and helplessness, in hope and defeated; my anger raged. Sometimes at my family, sometimes at myself, my spouse, other family members, and even at the situation in general. There were times I was angry that other people could not see my pain or even offer any solutions to my problem. I wanted someone to come in alongside of me and get in the trenches. I wanted answers, prayer warriors, miracles, and second chances.

I was not ready for this. I was unhappy with myself for all that I did not do, and all that was not done; Then the Calm. I knew that the damage had been done and at this point there was no more I could do. The line had been drawn in the sand, and I could no longer fight the good fight, I had to surrender. Still angry, sad and disappointed, I had to process the loss of my mother for what it was and move forward through life with some level of acceptance.

Can you identify your anger in relation to your loss?
_____
_____
_____
_____
_____

Can you identify all the persons or events that you may have directed your anger towards?
_____
_____
_____
_____
_____

Have you been able to process your anger in reference to your loss?_____
_____
_____
_____
_____
_____

After The Storm

Have you or are you willing to surrender your anger?
_____
_____
_____
_____

List ways you may deem helpful in moving forward, stepping out of anger into surrender and acceptance:
_____
_____
_____
_____

Phase 3 - Denial and Isolation: The Dream/Sequence Phase

This can't be real. This is not happening to me. I call this a Dream Sequence. Somehow, someway if this could by any chance be a dream, then I am ready to wake up and wake up now! However, you are so overwhelmed you do not sleep, nor eat, nor think clearly. When you start to face the reality of your situation and stop bargaining, and stop being angry, you may begin to deny how you really feel, or question that this is really the case at hand. I just knew that my mother was coming home. I knew that my mother's lungs were at the point that they had failed, but I had the hope that she could be like" Super Man"/Christopher Reeves. He could not breathe on his own and was given a permanent tracheotomy. I wanted that for my mother too! Sure he had lots of money and was famous, but he was no better than my mother. I was convinced it was due to her financial status in life, and was even told by nurses that she did not qualify for a transplant due to her age, weight, and financial status. Discrimination? Certainly! Maybe so, and Maybe not at all, but I was in this phase.

It was a New Year, and it was New Year's Day to be exact. My mom was just at my home for Christmas and she did not even stay her normal visit time...just twenty minutes. In the most inconspicuous and nonchalant way, she began to tell me she was going to be in the hospital for New Year's...She said she would have been there for Christmas, but she was holding out. Did she know? I am sure she did...My mom had been ill for some time and I am sure she had her moments of Denial. "I can beat this." " I am invincible." But I must say in the latter years I saw a tired, tattered and worn lady, trying to make it right, but still not quite getting the desired results and then **resignation.**

As I process this situation in my mind and face the reality of it all, over time my mom started to slowly decline in health and spirit. If I could pinpoint this down to an exact date I would say the decline started in September 2011 after her final visit to Duke Hospital in her quest for transplant surgery approval. She was filled with so much hope that this particular hospital would be the answer to her prayers. However, when she met with the Doctors, she was denied the surgery. I believe all hope was abandoned at this point and slowly acceptance and a then resignation, possibly due to her physical impairments, her emotional impairments or both. However, I do believe this date was the beginning of her transition to the end of her life becoming more of a reality to her. It may have been a reality that she had already accepted, and could not share with us, her family, or one that she just wanted to resist. The truth of this matter is that now we will never know, but we can learn and accept the situation that has transpired and choose to now move forward.

After The Storm

Can you identify ways in which you may have isolated yourself during or after your loss?
_____
_____
_____
_____
_____

Do did you began to deny this event was taking place? If so, can you list some of the ways in which denial played a part in reference to your loss?
_____
_____
_____
_____
_____

At any time during your occurrence with loss did you feel as if you were in a Dream Phase?
_____
_____
_____
_____
_____

Can you identify events that may have seemed like a dream like to you?
_____
_____
_____
_____
_____

In what ways have you began to come to some level of acceptance and began to move forward?
_____
_____
_____
_____
_____

After The Storm

What assisted you in the acceptance and moving forward process?
_____
_____
_____
_____
_____

And Now the Mourning

Mourning: A Period of Time of which outward signs of grief are shown.
(Per Webster's College Dictionary)

Part 2: Depression and Acceptance Phases 4 & 5

I allot this section exclusively to mourning because for me during my times of mourning I vacillated between periods of depression and acceptance as if somehow they were intertwined. After the decisions were made in regards to choosing to end the life of my mother; on some level I could logically receive all the issues at hand and understand the arguments being made by the medical professionals regarding her health. However, while wavering between accepting their logic, trying to process my emotions, and come to terms in regards to my faith and the sanctity of life, the outward signs of grief became overwhelming and undeniably evident as they presented in every area of my life.

There were times when I could not sleep, or eat. I would stay up all night and pray, and ask anyone who knew words of prayer to pray for a miracle for my mother. I even went through saying where there is life there is hope and as long as she was not brain dead, then she was still alive to me. After all was said and done, and the tubes were pulled and my mother was gone from this earth, the mourning process really began.

I once again moved through anger and isolation, as I became angry and easily agitated by the smallest things, when really I was hurt and unable to really process my feelings to reflect as such. The isolation began. I felt as if I was alone in this world. Even though my mother and I did not have a typical relationship, I always had not only the Hope of one day our relationship becoming what I wanted it to be, but the convenience of opportunity. I knew as long as she was alive there would be another opportunity to try all over again. When I would try to make things work between us and things did not transpire like I wanted them to, I would retreat and believe that once things blew over then I could try again. This became a vicious cycle between us both. Due to many unresolved issues between us, we at times had issues showing our true feelings towards each other. However, now that she was gone the opportunity for tomorrow was no longer a possibility and I was left holding on.

While researching this topic of Grief and Grief related Depression, I learned that experts say there are two types of depression in relation to this issue. It is believed that the main types of depression associated with grief are filled with sadness and regret coupled with a private type of depression in which we resign to an internal preparation process as we come to terms with saying good bye to our loved ones.

After The Storm

I must admit, I experienced those types of depression described above and more. There were days after my mother passed that the slightest little thing would send me into a stream of tears. The sight of an Ambulance, or even a song on the radio, would move me to great sadness, and then other times nothing at all. I could sometimes go through the day and think about her without any reactions of sadness at all. Sometimes I could even think about her and smile. All I knew was that I wanted it to stop. I wanted the tears to dry up and the pain to go away. I wanted to no longer feel like a stranger on this planet. I wanted to still feel as if I belonged to someone. I wanted my mother back. I always wanted her, even when we were at odds with each other, I wanted her and I am so grateful before she passed, I had the opportunity to express that to her while letting her know, God wanted her more. I felt it necessary to only bid my mother love and release her so when she vacated this plane she could leave in peace.

Can you identify with any of the issues presented in this section?
_____
_____
_____
_____

Are you able to list ways in which you may have come to grips logically with your loss, but not emotionally, and how does your Faith/Religious Convictions play a role?
_____
_____
_____
_____

Do you think your sadness or grief has lasted longer than you want it too?
_____
_____
_____
_____

After The Storm

Are you seeking professional help for your loss via (medical/religious/support groups) and do you know what is available in your area?_____

_____

_____

_____

Have you come to the realization that you are not your loss? This is something that has happened and is not the total sum definition of who you are although it might be a defining moment in your life.

_____

_____

_____

_____

Accepting my mother's Death is not something I have totally been able to come to terms with. I have accepted and moved on to some degree, but Acceptance seems to come in stages. I know the reality is that she is gone, and I know she is not coming back, but I still have issues overcoming the possibility of what could have been. The only thing I can accept is that God is Sovereign and that there must be a purpose for this to have transpired. With this concept **After the Storm** was birthed, and hopefully this will help those of you who are going through issues such as myself, have a reference point of identification, as well as an assurance that you are not alone.

Have you been able to fully accept your loss?

_____

_____

_____

_____

Is there still pain associated with the memory of your loss?

_____

_____

_____

_____

After The Storm

How are you coping with your loss (religion/faith/friends and family/professional help/support groups)?

_____
_____
_____
_____
_____

Are you able to associate your loss and your purpose?

_____
_____
_____
_____
_____

Are you substituting activities/things/or people (like shopping/over or under socializing) to cover up or defer (mask) the pain of your loss?

_____
_____
_____
_____

Would you define your activities that you are using if any, to cover up your pain negative or positive in nature, and how are they helpful to you?

_____
_____
_____

After The Storm

My Experience With Palliative Care:

From my understanding of Palliative Care as defined by the World Health Organization is that this type of care is an approach that aims to improves the quality of life of for the patients and their families who are faced with the complications of a life-threatening illness, by offering pain management to limit suffering, by means of early identification, assessment, and treatment of pain and other problems be it Spiritual, Physical, or Psychosocial (mind/humanity).

My Understanding of Palliative care during the event of my loss.

For Me Palliative care represented something that was extremely not palatable. I was being faced with life and death issues concerning someone who had given me life. Knowing my mother, I knew how much she wanted to live, and I was on her side. I could not choose this for her. I was not aware of her choosing this for herself either as she did not have a DNR in place (Do Not Resuscitate). My mother, who could barely breathe even while on the maximum amount of oxygen was still fighting for her life, and even after the removal of the ventilator tube she still attempted to escape her impending death by trying to get up off of her hospital bed. Palliative? Not for me, not at that point. However looking back, the issue of death is not Palatable. It is ugly and hard. It is harsh and grotesque. The palliative care team with all of their assistance was trying to help us accept the unacceptable. I was not ready for this; I never expected to see my mother in such a condition. When I saw my mother I saw myself, and I was determined that day to make her life and my life count. I was determined to tell our story and help others who may not know anything about this part of life. Death and dying with dignity while assisting the love ones come to terms with the impending loss; I believe is what palliative care was ultimately designed to do. However, I had a hard time with it all.

Through Research I have found palliative care to be defined in several different ways such as care that alleviates pain and symptoms without offering any additional support to the patient or their family. Care for people who were dying of cancer and who not or could not be treated any longer for their disease, which after the 1960's was extended to include all persons facing terminal illness. Then by the 1980's palliative care extended its scope to include not only care for the patient and the family but to include all persons that mattered to the patient; friends, family and loved ones blood or non-blood related. The latter was a provision implemented due to the impact of the AIDS epidemic.

The Umbrella of Terms

Other terms I found to fall under the umbrella of Palliative care were hospice care (at home or clinical based care for individuals suffering from debilitating or terminal conditions/illnesses), supportive care (usually provided to a patient and the patient's family from the time of diagnosis of a terminal illness, while treatment is being issued, and even in and after death during the bereavement process), and End of life care(pain management/care that is offered when it is determined that the patient will not survive their illness and the maximum level of treatment has been issued). By professional definition they may all differ technically, but to an average person such as me they all intertwine and are co-mingled at the end of your loved one's life. Once the diagnosis of a terminal illness is passed down to your loved one a whole new set of issues come to play. The purpose of this discussion/information is to help you in opening the doorway to the topics that will be at hand when faced with choosing life or impending death. While I was facing this issue with my mother I was unaware of all of these terms and even the degree of her illness, but today you have a chance to start from this very moment. There is no better time than the present to learn, love, heal, grow, and live each day as if it could be your last, because just might be!

From what I have read about the Founder of the Hospice Movement **Dame Cicely Mary Saunders**, was her approach to this whole type of care was that people mattered just because they existed. Her goal was to assist people who found themselves in this state to die not only with peace and dignity, but to enjoy life until death.

This is also my take away of the term Palliative Care as a whole. It is a care being offered to patients and their loved ones who are trying to navigate the complexities of illness, diagnosis, and treatment of a terminal illness or debilitating condition that could prove to be fatal. While letting the individuals know they matter. However, in doing just that, I feel people in need of this type of care should enjoy each day of their lives that remain to the fullest, without regrets.

If you or a loved one is faced with the need for this type of care do you have a Medical Directive in place or a DNR Living/ Will? Who may be a good candidate for this position in your life?

_____
_____
_____
_____

Do you clearly understand your condition or the condition of your love one and the possible treatment or possibility of the point when treatment is no longer an option?

_____
_____
_____
_____

After The Storm

Are you aware of help available to you in your area and how to access it?
_____
_____
_____
_____

Do You Know How to avoid or prepare so that an end of life event will not result in conflict for you?
(Faith/Family/Moral Structure/Cultural Bias/Medical/treatment Preference)
_____
_____
_____
_____

Recovering Emotionally After Loss

Facing issues Such as: The **death of a loved one**, the **end of a relationship** such as separation or divorce, major **health issues, miscarriage**, or major **financial changes** are all associated with loss. Grief is a normal reaction to these types of losses. In the world we live in today we are not necessarily equipped or educated on how to cope or recover from such situations and find ourselves unprepared when facing these issues. Moving forward can present itself with many challenges while trying to gain control of our emotions. You may experience people offering you words of comfort by telling you "it will be ok", or "time heals all wounds", or "keep yourself busy", or "that person was no good any way". However, all these statements sound good in passing, but the reality is that without the proper tools moving forward can seem a daunting task. In this phase it is best to seek professional help, be it spiritual with a clergyman/woman of your choice, or with professional counselor.

Getting the Help You Need
Gaining access to the tools needed to move forward is more beneficial than trading the devil for the witch. Moving on is dependent on what you are moving to, or in letting go of. If you let go of one thing and then pick up a replica of your last experience to help you cope with your grief, you are not recovering at all. You are just masking the pain and putting calluses on your heart. If you knew how to let go or move on, you would have already done so. With all that being said, reaching outside of yourself would bring you the most optimal result.

The relief you are seeking may not come all at once, or never totally, but you could possibly gain the skills to help you manage. Your goal should be to know there is life after loss and to get to a place where the memory no longer causes pain for you. The outcome and process to reach this level of recovery may be different for each individual as is the many situations that present themselves in reference to loss. However, for me I had to keep reminding myself that my mother had passed, and I was still alive. I had to keep living. I had to choose a way to honor the memory of my mother and move forward in a positive light while trying to heal. It is always best when facing issues such as loss to take care of yourself and keep an open line of communication in a safe environment with someone you trust. It is never good to stuff your feelings and or emotions as that could lead to further issues with deeper consequences such as addictions, or deeper stages of depression.

After The Storm

Helpful Tips

Some helpful tips to aid in your process of moving forward would be to **avoid isolating from others.** Spending too much time alone could possibly make the overwhelming emotions surrounding your loss appear greater. Staying connected to family and friends, finding a Support Group, as well as attending your normal activities and events could all work together in the process of healing.

For me I went back to work immediately and attended church regularly. Sticking to a regular routine helped me get back to what most will call normal. I still had my days when thoughts would run across my mind and tears would flow, but I cried and made forward movements. The key is to keep moving. I also tried to keep regular eating and sleeping habits as much as possible. I just wanted to find my *new normal*. In finding my *new normal,* a new purpose and passion was born. I decided that to help myself I had to help others and that is how this workshop *After the Storm* was developed. I found old friends were readily available to offer comfort and sound advice as well as share their stories. These things are still a work in progress for me. There are days when I have to resist isolating myself and push past the desire to be complacent. However, I must remember I am still among the living and I am not my loss. I must move on and I encourage you to find something that motivates you to reach out beyond yourself and move forward in your healing.

Make Time for Yourself

Another important tip in your process of recovery will be to **make time for yourself** and the things you enjoy. If you enjoy a quality hair style, then make sure you keep your appearance up. Get a manicure or pedicure. You may find these activities not only physically enhancing but they may help in the reduction of stress. Also making sure you get plenty of rest will be crucial in helping you maintain your emotional balance. I know all things seem better to me after a good night's sleep. Exercise, something I am still working on, has been documented to be a good tool in the emotional healing process as well. It is reported that regular exercise releases chemicals in your brain that are call endorphins and will aid in the process of maintaining regular sleep habits. It is also reported that the healthier you are, the happier you can become as a healthy body helps reduce the emotional stresses of loss.

After The Storm

Keep the lines of Communication Open

Keeping lines of communication open can also be a helpful tool when trying to recover from the stress of loss. For the person who is listening, it is best not to offer too much advice and not to judge the thought and feelings of the person who is expressing their emotions. A listening and understanding ear is always appreciated. Being mindful that the situation that this person is going through does not have to be perceived as rational to you, be supportive and show love and concern. Also be aware of what they are saying, if it seems that they are in a place that maybe self-destructive or destructive to others you may want to point them in the direction of professional services as their situation may deem it necessary.

Don't Lay Blame

Most of all don't lay blame. **Blaming only keeps the wounds open**. I have attended many church services and truly believe the scripture which says that we must forgive so that our father in heaven will forgive us as well. There is healing in forgiveness, not so much for the person you may be angry with but for you. If by some chance you are blaming yourself you should know self-blame is self-destructive. If blame is an issue you cannot overcome, help from a support group, or a clergy member may be in order to help you with the principles of forgiveness. In my particular situation, blame was easy to place on myself and on all of the other parties involved even on my mother for so many reasons. However, the real truth is that at the end of it all, the blame did not matter, I loved her and she loved me, and I needed her to know that before she passed as well as her needing to hear it. Even after her death blame could have been placed, but was defeating and not healing; my goal in this life is to aim towards things which attract higher levels of energy. Blame and un-forgiveness are all low level energy actions. I found for me to recover I had to reach to things that pulled me out and not down. Ultimately, we should be seeking to remove the issues surrounding our unresolved conflicts, work at resolving them, and show love while doing so.

Honesty

Honesty is the best policy. We must first be **honest with ourselves** by ascertaining what it is that we really want, not only out of life, but out of our relationships. If we are really honest with ourselves at the core of our list it would all equate to *love*. After all was said and done and I truly came clean with myself, I realized that despite all of the differences between my mother and myself, and with all the people in my life at the core of it all I wanted their love; Unconditional, unreserved, and unprejudiced.

After The Storm

Being honest is not always our go to character trait because within the realm of honesty other factors start to come into play such as vulnerability and the fear of rejection. Most of us do not get what we really want because of these two factors. The average person does not fundamentally start out operating in ways that are not honest or deceitful, but over time have learned this behavior to be rewarding for them. You may ask what the reward is. Well, the reward is protection. We live in a blanket of dishonesty to protect ourselves from what we may consider to be many things, but truly it is because we are trapped in fear. Fear of the unknown, Fear of rejection, and Fear of being vulnerable.

These fears are not unwarranted, as for myself I have found in many instances when I let my guard down and ask for help it falls on deaf ears. I have found that it takes very special people to want to get involved in your struggles, and that the reality of that is they can only get in but so far. Once again in our need to protect ourselves we put up shields. I have them. Mine look like, "I'm Fine" or "I will manage" when I really want to say *Help Me*. However on the other hand, in my times of requesting help I have found that once again, people can only help you but so much. The decision has to be made in your own mind to reach outside of yourself, to really seek. For those of you who are of Christian background you would be familiar with seeking first the Kingdom of God. And for those who are more universal in nature you would seek your higher power, but, for those of you who may not identify with any religious or universal theory you may need to consult professionals in your area or talk with family or friends, but seek, there is hope, and the hope is that we can get the help we are looking for.

Give up the need to be right

Due to the events that surrounded the death of my mother I realized that giving up the need to be right was my take away from this whole event. I had realized I was guilty of placing more value on my need to be right than on the more ultimate issue of wanting and desiring my mother's love. I allowed too much time to pass between differences due to the stance; I took on what I felt were wrongs she committed against me. In operating in this fashion we can always find people who will tell us we are right in feeling the way we feel, or doing the things we do. But we must go back to being honest. Is this really helping you in getting what you really want? We all ultimately want to be loved. So we must decide, do we want to be right more than we want to be loved, or is our need to be right more valuable than the relationship that this scenario may find itself playing out in. Now please do not take this to the extreme and stay in any abusive situations. This matter is for practicality, and there will be other factors at play in your decision. However, this is just food for thought the next time you let too much time pass between the fall outs or disagreements between you and a person you love.

After The Storm

Emotional Healing Worksheet

Are you able to identify where you are in reference to your emotional healing process surrounding your loss?

_____
_____
_____
_____

Is the event of your loss something that has just recently happened? Or has several years passed?

_____
_____
_____
_____

Are you considering getting any type of help outside of yourself?

_____
_____
_____
_____

Can you identify who (person) or what (organization) you may be comfortable reaching out to?

_____
_____
_____
_____

Are you aware of the services available to you in your area?

_____
_____
_____
_____

Can you identify at least one person who you trust that will commit to you on a weekly basis just so you can talk freely surrounding the events of your loss and your emotions?

_____
_____
_____

After The Storm

Can you relate to the information provided on blaming, and can you identify who you may be blaming and associate the blame you are placing on that particular person or set of events?

_____
_____
_____
_____

Can you identify any unresolved issues between you and a loved one, and can you detail what measures you are currently taking or hope to take in the resolution of your conflict?

_____
_____
_____
_____

Can you identify what has more value to you, the need to be right or the need to be loved?

_____
_____
_____
_____

Are you able to detail some things that you have discontinued doing since your loss that you would have never stopped if the event surrounding your loss never happened?

_____
_____
_____
_____

Are you willing to make a commitment to yourself that you will attempt to begin to do some of the things that you have detailed in the above question again? And if not, will you attempt to try and find new positive outlets that will bring you joy?

_____
_____
_____
_____

After The Storm

Did you find this workbook to be helpful, and would you like to attend *"After The Storm II" Removing the Lie!*?

_____
_____
_____
_____

I encourage you to continue to journal your thoughts and feelings as this may produce some level of comfort as well as some sort of road map to your feelings. If nothing more hopefully it will help you in opening a discussion between you and a loved one, or professional in your community so that you can begin to bring healing to the emotions that hurt.

Helpful Reading:

Ref: National cancer control programmes: policies and managerial guidelines, 2nd ed. Geneva, World Health Organization, 2002. www.who.int/cancer

Elisabeth Kübler-Ross, M.D. (July 8, 1926 – August 24, 2004) author of: *On Death and Dying* (1969)

www.cicelysaundersfoundation.org/ Founder of the Hospice Movement

The Curse Breaker Being Made by God by T. B. Williams

About The Author

T. B. Williams is an Author/Publisher/Radio Personality and Documentary Film Maker.

To contact T. B. Williams for speaking engagements or to set up a workshop for your organization you can e-mail or write to:

FBT/MBSS PRODUCTIONS, LLC

E-mail address: contactus@upandcomingtoday.com

Or by traditional mail: P. O. Box 3066, Newport News VA, 23603

After The Storm

Journal

After The Storm

Journal

After The Storm

Journal

After The Storm

Journal

After The Storm

Journal

After The Storm

Journal

After The Storm

Journal

After The Storm

Journal

After The Storm

Journal

After The Storm

Journal

After The Storm

Journal

After The Storm

Journal

After The Storm

Journal

After The Storm

Journal